THE MAC ATTACK

THE ROAD TO 62
AND BEYOND!

Trade Life Books
Tulsa, Oklahoma

The Mac Attack:
The Road to 62 and Beyond!
ISBN 1-57757-062-6
Copyright © 1998 by Trade Life Books
P.O. Box 55325
Tulsa, Oklahoma 74155

Cover and text design/layout: Paragon Communications Group, Inc., Tulsa, OK

Cover Photo: © 1998 Allsport USA/Stephen Dunn. All rights reserved.

Not authorized or endorsed by Mark McGwire

THE
MAC
ATTACK

THE ROAD TO 62
AND BEYOND!

DEDICATION

- To the incredible fans of America's favorite sport.

- To boys and girls everywhere—
  never give up on your dreams.

- To the Mark McGwire Charitable Foundation—
  for the work you do with children.

- To home run ball number 62—
  What a ride!

INTRODUCTION

HE DID IT!

When Babe Ruth hit 60 home runs in 1927, he dared anyone to break his record.

Thirty-four years later, in 1961, Roger Maris did just that.

Neither The Babe nor Maris were seriously challenged until 1997, when McGwire hit 58 homers.

But on September 9, 1998, after thirty-seven years of waiting, before 43,688 screaming fans, McGwire set a new standard for home run hitters.

The Mac Attack is the story of his road to 62 . . . and beyond!

THE WEAPON OF CHOICE

WHAT DOES McGWIRE CARRY INTO BATTLE WITH HIM?

His bat is a 34 1/2-inch, 33-ounce Rawlings Big Stick, known officially as the MACZS. The barrel is 10 inches long and 2-inches wide. With a handle of only 3 1/2 inches in circumference, he breaks a dozen bats each month of the season.

He breaks the heart of at least that many pitchers!

AMERICAN LEGION HERO

Near the end of his senior year in high school, McGwire was diagnosed with appendicitis and mononucleosis. He missed the first several weeks of his American Legion season with Claremont, and wasn't able to get into pitching shape. As a result, he had to play first base the entire summer. He led Claremont to the state playoffs in California with a .415 batting average, 14 home runs, and 53 runs batted in.

McGWIRE BY THE NUMBERS

NAME:	Mark David McGwire
BIRTHDATE:	October 1, 1963
BIRTHPLACE:	Pomona, California
HOME:	Alamo, California
FAMILY:	One son, Matthew, age 10; single
HEIGHT:	6'5"
WEIGHT:	250 pounds
DRAFTED:	Selected by the Oakland Athletics in 1984

POSITION:	First Base
UNIFORM NUMBER:	25
BATS:	Right
THROWS:	Right
SEASONS PLAYED:	11
FORMER TEAMS:	Oakland Athletics, 1986-1997
CURRENT TEAM:	St. Louis Cardinals; signed through 2000
ACQUIRED:	Trade with the Oakland A's, for pitchers T. J. Mathews, Eric Ludwick, and Blake Stein, July 31, 1997

IN THE BEGINNING

Mark David McGwire was born in Pomona, California, on October 1, 1963. He is the third of five brothers. As grown ups, the McGwire boys now range in height from 6'2" to 6'8". Mark, at 6'5", is right in the middle. Younger brother, Dan, was a star quarterback in college for the University of Iowa and San Diego State, and played in the NFL for the Seattle Seahawks.

ROOKIE RECORD

Because of his home run prowess, McGwire has always commanded much media attention. In 1987, his first full year in the majors, the big question from reporters was whether he could break Al Rosen's record for homers by a rookie—38—set in 1950 with the Cleveland Indians.

On August 14, 1987, McGwire bested Rosen, going on to hit 49 for the season. Questions about the possibility of his breaking Maris' record never stopped coming after that.

ROAD TO 62  AND BEYOND

SIZING UP McGWIRE

McGwire is 6'5" and 250 pounds, with 17-inch forearms, 19-inch biceps, and some of the widest shoulders to ever play Major League Baseball. But his waist is only an enviable 32 inches. Perhaps the most significant number is five: McGwire has less than five percent body fat.

His secret? During the off season, he lifts weights six days a week for two hours. During the regular season, he lifts weights a half hour, three times per week.

VERY INTELLIGENT

"I always have had a saying, 'Show me the parents and I'll tell you who you are.' He has great parents. He and his dad and I went to a ball game, and Mark impressed me with his personality and he was very intelligent. I told him he was a USC kind of athlete."

—Rod Dedeaux
McGwire's coach at USC

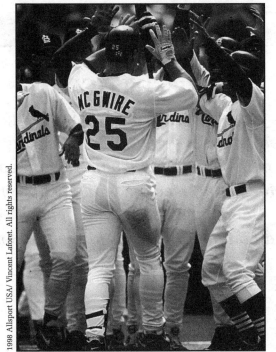

McGwire's teammates congratulate him after another round tripper.

NEVER BIG-HEADED

"I've never felt that Mark was ever as impressed
with his success in sports as other people.
Aware of it, yes, but never big-headed about it.
I've always assumed that we were like most families—
that we tried to teach our kids the importance of always
doing their best, being polite, and respecting people."

—Ginger McGwire
Mark's Mother

A SILVER YEAR

In 1984, McGwire played for the University of Southern California Trojans, where he was a teammate with strikeout pitcher, Randy Johnson, now of the Houston Astros. McGwire, who had aspirations of being a pitcher himself, moved to first base on a full-time basis after his freshman year of college. He hit 32 home runs in 67 games for the Trojans, a single-season mark that equals USC's career record. That summer, McGwire played on the U.S. squad that won the silver medal at the Los Angeles Olympics.

BASH BROTHERS

In 1987, McGwire became teammate to Jose Canseco, the 1986 rookie of the year, and the two became known as the "Bash Brothers." They terrorized opposing pitchers and led Oakland to American League pennants for three straight years (1988-90) and a World Series victory in 1989. They picked up their nickname because of the way they would "bash" their forearms together after homers.

DAMIEN HIGH

McGwire transferred to Damien High School, an all-boys Catholic school, midway through his freshman year. A much smaller school than what he had been attending, he felt it gave him a better opportunity to play sports.

He didn't make varsity baseball until his junior year when he batted .359. He also pitched, and had a 5-3 record, with a 1.90 earned-run average.

MAC ATTACKS

First player to hit more than 50 home runs in three consecutive seasons: 1996, 1997, 1998

Reached 400 home runs in fewest at-bats in Major League history, 4,726, besting the previous best of 4,854, by Babe Ruth

Golden Glove in 1990

Selected to All-Star team 10 times

Best home runs to At-Bats ratio among all players
(11.3 At-Bats/HRs)

COLLEGE ADDED UP

The Montreal Expos selected McGwire in the eighth round of the 1981 baseball draft, and offered him a signing bonus of $8,500. McGwire had been considering a move straight from high school to professional baseball. But when he did the math, he figured the scholarship offer to University of Southern California was worth at least $50 thousand. Go figure!

THE RACE TO 400

McGwire reached 400 home runs in fewer At-Bats than any man in baseball history!

Mark McGwire 4,726

Babe Ruth 4,854

Harmon Killebrew 5,300

Willie McCovey 5,751

Jimmie Foxx 5,774

Mike Schmidt 5,790

O A D T O 6 2 A N D B E Y O N D

MARCH MADNESS—1998
THE RACE IS ON!

Mark McGwire hits number 1 for the year!

AB	H	HR	RBI	BB	AVG
4	2	1	4	0	.500

Mac didn't waste any time pursuing Maris' record. On March 31, 1998, McGwire became the only player in Cardinal history to hit a Grand Slam on opening day. It was his 10th career Grand Slam.

TEE TIME!

McGwire quit baseball during his sophmore year of high school and switched to the golf team. He had a pulled muscle in his chest at the time and couldn't swing the bat right. Plus he was playing junior varsity, which had him discouraged. But he couldn't stay away from baseball too long, and was a starter on the varsity team at Damien High his junior year.

McGWIRE'S TOP VICTIMS

10 Longest Home Runs

DATE	PITCHER	TEAM	FEET
5/16/98	Livan Hernandez	Florida	545
6/24/97	Randy Johnson	Seattle	538
5/12/98	Paul Wagner	Milwaukee	527
9/16/97	Ramon Martinez	Los Angeles	517
4/20/97	Brian Moehler	Detroit	514
8/26/98	Justin Speier	Florida	510
9/2/97	Jaime Navarro	Chicago White Sox	504
8/30/98	Dennis Martinez	Atlanta	501
8/22/97	Tony Saunders	Florida	500
7/25/96	Huck Flener	Toronto	488

Top 10 Teams

HOMERS	TEAM
40	Detroit Tigers
35	Boston Red Sox
31	Texas Rangers
30	Baltimore Orioles
30	Minnesota Twins
29	Anaheim Angels
28	Cleveland Indians
27	Chicago White Sox
26	Kansas City Royals
24	New York Yankees

Through 1997

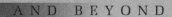
Top 6 Pitchers

HOMERS	PITCHER
7	Frank Tanana
6	Jim Abbott
5	Eric King
5	Scott Erickson
5	Tom Gordon
5	Mark Langston

Through 1997

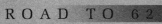
Top 5 Ballparks

NO.	BALLPARK
166	Oakland-Alameda County Coliseum (Oakland)
31	Busch Stadium (St. Louis)
23	Tiger Stadium (Detroit)
18	Fenway Park (Boston)
15	Yankee Stadium (New York Yankees)

Through 1997

POWERQUOTES

CRY BABY

Why did McGwire's father refuse to let him play Little League baseball at age seven?

"I'd heard too much about arguing, meddling parents and bad coaches. I didn't want anybody to screw up my son. When I told him he couldn't play, he cried and cried and cried."

—John McGwire

ALASKAN SUMMER

McGwire went to USC with high hopes of being a star pitcher. In fact, as a freshman, 20 of his 29 appearances were as a pitcher. But Ron Vaughn, a USC assistant coach, asked McGwire to come play summer league ball in Alaska with him during the summer 1982—as a first baseman. Despite hesitations—and after battling intense home sickness—McGwire led the Anchorage Glacier Pilots with a .403 batting average, 13 home runs, and 53 runs batted in.

Even batting practice draws a crowd when McGwire is at bat.

POWERQUOTES

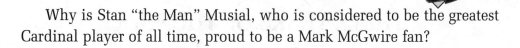

Why is Stan "the Man" Musial, who is considered to be the greatest Cardinal player of all time, proud to be a Mark McGwire fan?

"It's a combination of reasons. He has so much talent, but he's also a darn nice guy. To see him in St. Louis playing for the Cardinals and treating people the way he does, I'm really pleased. I think he has a good chance of breaking the record. I'd love to see it happen."

THREE YEARS OF THUNDER

McGwire's home run parade that began in 1996, has reached epic proportions. No one in the history of Major League Baseball, not even Babe Ruth, has had such an awesome display of power over this extended period of time.

The following chart shows the best three year totals ever.

YEARS	PLAYER	HR	GAMES
1996-98	Mark McGwire	172*	480*
1926-28	Babe Ruth	161	457
1927-29	Babe Ruth	160	440
1932-34	Jimmie Foxx	150	453
1928-30	Babe Ruth	149	434
1920-22	Babe Ruth	128	404

*through September 8, 1998

Mac attacks the ball at Chicago's Wrigley Field.

POWERQUOTES

GOING FISHING

"I used to love to come to the ballpark.
Now I hate it. Every day becomes a little tougher
because of all this. Writers, tape recorders, microphones,
cameras, questions and more questions.
Roger Maris lost his hair the season he hit sixty-one.
I still have all my hair, but when it's over,
I'm going home to Mobile and fish
for a long time."

—Hank Aaron

(on his march to break Babe Ruth's career record of 714 home runs)

OFFICER McGWIRE?

McGwire, whose father, John, is a dentist, and whose mother, Ginger, is a homemaker and community volunteer, at one time considered a career in law enforcement.

The appeal?

"They do the same thing every day, but it's different because they don't know what to expect. It's a lot like baseball."

A STAR IS BORN

Are home run hitters born to be sluggers—or are they made that way through great coaching and hard work? For McGwire, the answer might be "yes" to both options. In 1971, eight-year-old Mark nailed a home run over the right field fence in his first official Little League At-Bat—against a twelve-year-old pitcher. Within three years he set the Claremont, California, Little League record for home runs. His 1974 tally of 13 dingers stood for twenty years.

FIRST THINGS FIRST

On October 4, 1987, having already hit 49 home runs for the season, McGwire gave up a shot to hit 50 homers so he could be present for the birth of his first-born child. He skipped the final game of the season to be with his wife, Kathy, when she gave birth to Matthew, who is currently the bat boy for the St. Louis Cardinals. Some fans and sports writers questioned his decision not to play. But McGwire reasoned that while there would be many more chances to hit 50 home runs, he would have only one first-born child in his lifetime.

He was right!

TAKE OUT THE TRASH?

"As a boy, he'd lay on the floor watching baseball games on television. He wouldn't take the trash out as long as there was a game on. He always had that dream of playing in the major leagues."

—Ginger McGwire, Mark's mother

A MILLION DOLLAR BALL?

The Shop at Home television network began bidding at $250,000 for home run ball number 62. By September 8, two groups were offering $1 million to the fan who captured McGwire's historic blast.

However, when groundskeeper Tim Forneris nabbed number 62, he immediately turned the ball over to McGwire without asking for a cent.

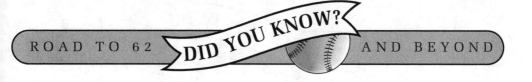
A DATE TO REMEMBER

Maris hit home run number 61 on October 1, 1961. Two years later in 1963, on the same day of the year, a young man named Mark McGwire was born in Ponoma, California.

* THE ASTERISK

When Maris began to make a run at Ruth, he was scorned, first by the game's establishment and then by the fans. He hit his 35th homer on July 15—putting him 19 games ahead of Ruth's pace.

At that point, baseball's commissioner, Ford Frick, an old friend of Ruth, declared that for the record to be officially broken, it would have to happen in 154 games—the length of Ruth's season.

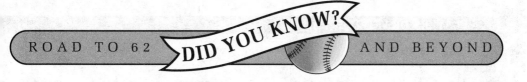

A 1998 ALL-STAR

McGwire became a Major League All-Star for the tenth time in 1998, leading the National League in votes with 3,377,145 fans voting him in as the starting first baseman. 1998 was his first year as a National Leaguer. He started six out of the nine years he made the squad in the American League.

Ironically, McGwire has never hit a homer in an All-Star game. All four of his hits have been singles.

1984 Draft

No	Player	Team	Position	Career Highlights
1	Shawn Abner	New York Mets	Outfielder	Traded to San Diego, where he began a six-year career that ended with a .227 batting average.
2	Bill Swift	Seattle	Pitcher	He's in his 13th big-league season. After time with San Francisco and Colorado, he's back with Seattle.
3	Drew Hall	Chicago Cubs	Pitcher	He played five years with three teams, going 9-12.

PLAYERS DRAFTED AHEAD OF McGWIRE

No	Player	Team	Position	Career Highlights
4	Cory Snyder	Cleveland	Outfielder/Infielder	He hit 149 home runs in nine seasons, including 33 in 1987.
5	Pat Pacillo	Cincinnati	Pitcher	Pacillo was 4-3 in 18 starts in two seasons with the Reds.
6	Erik Pappas	California	Catcher	He played three years with the Cubs and Cardinals.
7	Mike Dunne	St. Louis	Pitcher	He was 25-30 in five seasons with four teams.

PLAYERS DRAFTED AHEAD OF McGWIRE

No	Player	Team	Position	Career Highlights
8	Jay Bell	Minnesota	Shortstop	He was traded for Bert Blyleven, who helped the Twins win the 1987 World Series. Bell homered on the first pitch he saw in the majors. It was from Blyleven. Plays for Arizona.
9	Alan Cockrell	San Francisco	Outfielder	He managed eight big-league At-Bats with Colorado in 1996.

BASEBALL STATS

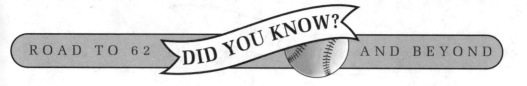
MARK AND TOMMY

When Tommy John, then of the New York Yankees, gave up Mark McGwire's first major league hit, a single, and then his second, a double, it wasn't the first time they met. McGwire's father, John, was Tommy John's dentist when he played for the California Angels, and their families became friends.

In 1985, after John had been cut by California, he attempted a comeback with the Athletic's Class A team in Modesto, California, where he was teammates with McGwire.

MARIS HIGHLIGHTS

- Was recruited by University of Oklahoma as a running back. When no one from the university met him at the train station, he returned to North Dakota.

- Made his debut for the Cleveland Indians on April 16, 1957.

- Traded to the Kansas City Athletics in 1958, and then on to the Yankees for the 1960 season.

ROGER MARIS

- Was American League MVP in 1960 with 39 home runs and a league-leading 112 RBIs. He barely nips Mickey Mantle for the award with 225-222 votes.

- Repeats as American League MVP in 1961, leading the league with 61 homers and 142 RBIs. Despite breaking Ruth's record, he again barely edges Mantle for the award, this time 202-198 in votes.

- Traded to the St. Louis Cardinals in 1967, where he played his final two seasons, appearing in two more World Series.

ROGER MARIS

BASEBALL STATS

TOP FIVE SLUGGERS
Career Home Run Ratio

For his career, McGwire hits one homer for every 11.3 times he is at bat—just ahead of Babe Ruth's ratio of 1/11.8.

PLAYER	HR	AB	RATIO
Mark McGwire	449	5,075	11.3
Babe Ruth	714	8,399	11.8
Ralph Kiner	369	5,205	14.1
Albert Belle	233	3,300	14.2
Harmon Killebrew	573	8,147	14.2

McGwire and Ruth dominate the 10 greatest seasons ever:

PLAYER, TEAM	YEAR	AB	HR	RATE
Mark McGwire, A's	1995	317	39	8.13
Mark McGwire, A's	1996	423	52	8.13
Babe Ruth, Yankees	1920	458	54	8.48
Babe Ruth, Yankees	1927	540	60	9.00
Babe Ruth, Yankees	1921	540	59	9.15
Mark McGwire, A's-Cards	1997	540	58	9.31
Mickey Mantle, Yankees	1961	514	54	9.52
Hank Greenberg, Tigers	1938	556	58	9.59
Roger Maris, Yankees	1961	590	61	9.67
Hank Aaron, Braves	1973	392	40	9.80

Through 1997

BASEBALL STATS

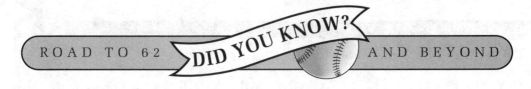
MARIS AND McGWIRE

There are actually several pitchers who either faced or were teamates with both Maris and McGwire.

Tommy John faced Maris many times and gave up McGwire's first major league hit.

Nolan Ryan struck out Maris twice and fanned McGwire six times. He also struck out Sammy Sosa eight times.

Phil Niekro faced Maris after he was traded to the Cardinals. In his last season, Neikro faced McGwire in his rookie year, and gave up one of McGwire's five career triples.

Steve Carlton played with Maris in 1967 and 1968, when the St. Louis Cardinals reached the World Series, and later pitched to McGwire.

THE "400 CLUB"

McGwire began 1998 with 387 home runs, and crashed his way into MLB's elite "400 Club" with a four-bagger off of Rick Reed of the Mets on May 8.

Hank Aaron	755
Babe Ruth	714
Willie Mays	660
Frank Robinson	586
Harmon Killebrew	573
Reggie Jackson	563
Mike Schmidt	548
Mickey Mantle	536
Jimmie Foxx	534
Willie McCovey	521
Ted Williams	521

Ernie Banks 512
Eddie Mathews. 512
Mel Ott. 511
Eddie Murray 501
Lou Gehrig 493
Stan Musial 475
Willie Stargell 475
Dave Winfield 465
Carl Yastrzemski. 452
Mark McGwire 449*
Dave Kingman 442
Andre Dawson 438
Billy Williams 426
Darrell Evans 414
Duke Snider 407

And counting!

HOME SWEET HOME

The baseball world was shocked when McGwire signed a three-year extension to play in St. Louis for about $8 million a year.

As an unrestricted free agent, he undoubtedly could have demanded much more money on the open market. Why stay?

The FANS.

"I had a great 11 years in Oakland and I thank them for that, but nothing like this ever happened," was his response to becoming the toast of the town.

AS BIG AS I CAN

"How to hit home runs: I swing as hard as I can, and I try to swing right through the ball. . . . The harder you grip the bat, the more you can swing it through the ball, and the farther the ball will go. I swing big, with everything I've got. I hit big or I miss big. I like to live as big as I can. . . . If I'd just tried for them dinky singles I could've batted around six hundred."

—Babe Ruth

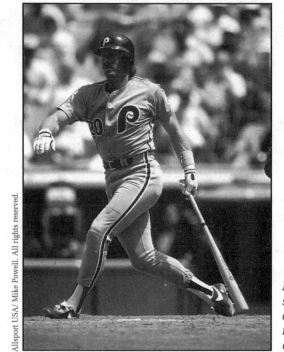

Mike Schmidt is seventh on the all-time home run list with 548 dingers.

McGWIRE IN THE POST SEASON

McGwire made it to the playoffs in five of his first seven years in Major League Baseball with the Oakland Athletics. He hit at least one home run in four different series, but his greatest moment came in 1989, as his A's swept the San Francisco Giants.

The following pages highlight McGwire's post-season play.

1988

American League Championship Series

Athletics sweep Red Sox, 4-0, as Dennis Eckersley saves all four games and is named the series MVP.

At-Bats	Hits	Average	Homers	RBIs	Walks	Strikeouts
15	5	.333	1	3	1	5

World Series

Dodgers down Athletics, 4-1, inspired by Kirk Gibson's "miraculous" pinch hit home run with two out in the bottom of the ninth inning off of Eckersley in Game 1.

At-Bats	Hits	Average	Homers	RBIs	Walks	Strikeouts
17	1	.059	1	1	3	4

1989

American League Championship Series

Athletics crush Blue Jays, 4-1, as Rickey Henderson hits .400 and steals 8 bases.

At-Bats	Hits	Average	Homers	RBIs	Walks	Strikeouts
18	7	.389	1	3	1	3

World Series

Oakland wins "Battle of the Bay" over San Francisco, 4-0. Game Three is postponed when an earthquake measuring 7.2 on the Richter Scale strikes twenty minutes before game time, damaging Candlestick Park and much of the Bay Area.

At-Bats	Hits	Average	Homers	RBIs	Walks	Strikeouts
17	5	.294	0	1	1	3

1990

American League Championship Series

Athletics rout Red Sox, 4-0, as Roger Clemens is ejected in the second inning of Game 4 for cursing at home plate umpire Terry Cooney.

At-Bats	Hits	Average	Homers	RBIs	Walks	Strikeouts
13	2	.154	0	2	3	3

World Series

Cincinnati Reds stun the highly favored A's, 4-0, behind the pitching of Jose Rijo (series MVP), and the hitting of Chris Sabo.

At-Bats	Hits	Average	Homers	RBIs	Walks	Strikeouts
14	3	.214	0	0	2	4

1992

American League Championship Series

Blue Jays defeat A's 4-2, avenging their loss of 1989, and officially ending Oakland's "dynasty."

At-Bats	Hits	Average	Homers	RBIs	Walks	Strikeouts
20	3	.150	1	3	5	4

AND HE SELLS NEWSPAPERS, TOO!

It is estimated that every time McGwire hits a home run, the *St. Louis Post-Dispatch* sells an extra 2,000 newspapers the next day. Circulation jumped by 7,000 newspapers the day after he hit three home runs against Philadelphia on May 19, 1998.

*Reggie Jackson
hits one of his
563 career
home runs.*

RBIs

1.	Hank Aaron	2,297	6.	Jimmie Foxx	1,922
2.	Babe Ruth	2,213	7.	Willie Mays	1,903
3.	Lou Gehrig	1,995	8.	Eddie Murray	1,899
4.	Stan Musial	1,951	9.	Cap Anson	1,879
5.	Ty Cobb	1,937	10.	Mel Ott	1,860

BASEBALL STATS

POWERQUOTES

A MOVING BUS

"Anything coming that way from him, you're definitely going to react. I don't think anybody wants to get hit by him. That's like saying you're going to go out in the middle of the interstate and stand in front of a bus."

—John Hudek

(The Cincinnati Reds relief pitcher made this statement in the news conference after McGwire hit a smash up the middle with Hudek pitching to him on September 6, 1998. Hudek had hit the ground hard to avoid getting hit.)

THE "50 HOMER" CLUB

In 1996, McGwire joined 16 other men who have hit more than 50 home runs in a single season. McGwire will attempt to join Ruth as the only other man to have passed that milestone in four different seasons in 1999.

YEAR	PLAYER	TEAM	NUMBER
1998	Mark McGwire	Cardinals	62*
1961	Roger Maris	Yankees	61
1927	Babe Ruth	Yankees	60
1921	Babe Ruth	Yankees	59
1932	Jimmy Foxx	A's	58
1938	Hank Greenberg	Tigers	58
1997	Mark McGwire	A's & Cards	58
1998	Sammy Sosa	Cubs	58*
1997	Ken Griffey Jr.	Mariners	56
1930	Hack Wilson	Cubs	56

*And counting!

YEAR	PLAYER	TEAM	NUMBER
1949	Ralph Kiner	Pirates	54
1961	Mickey Mantle	Yankees	54
1920	Babe Ruth	Yankees	54
1928	Babe Ruth	Yankees	54
1977	George Foster	Reds	52
1956	Mickey Mantle	Yankees	52
1965	Willie Mays	Giants	52
1996	Mark McGwire	A's	52

YEAR	PLAYER	TEAM	NUMBER
1990	Cecil Fielder	Tigers	51
1947	Ralph Kiner	Pirates	51
1955	Willie Mays	Giants	51
1947	Johnny Mize	Giants	51
1996	Brady Anderson	Baltimore	50
1995	Albert Belle	Indians	50
1938	Jimmy Foxx	Red Sox	50

MAC'S HOMERS OF DISTINCTION

- McGwire's first major league homer is hit against Walt Terrell at Detroit, on August 25, 1986.

- McGwire slams his 39th homer of the 1987 season on August 14, against Don Sutton of the California Angels, to break the existing record for homers in a rookie season.

- McGwire goes on to hit a total of 49 homers in his first year in the majors, setting a new, seemingly unbreakable mark.

- McGwire hit his first Grand Slam in the majors on August 11, 1988, against California's DeWayne Buice.

MILESTONE HOME RUNS

- McGwire reaches the 100 home run mark on July 5, 1989, against Charlie Leibrandt of the Kansas City Royals. He did it in less bats than any man except Ralph Kiner.

- McGwire smacks number 200 on June 10, 1992, against Milwaukee's Chris Bosio.

- McGwire hits homers number 300 and 301 on June 25, against Detroit, becoming the 73rd Major League player to reach that milestone.

- McGwire sets record of homers for an Athletic with 303, on July 2, 1996, breaking Jimmie Foxx's record set when the club was in Philadelphia.

MILESTONE HOME RUNS

- McGwire hits 52 home runs in 1996.

- McGwire begins the 1998 season with a home run in each of the first four games—matching Willie May's previous record.

- McGwire hits the longest homer of his career, and the longest ever recorded in Busch Stadium, measured at 545 feet, against Livan Hernandez of the Marlins on May 16, 1998.

- McGwire reaches 400 home runs in fewer times At-Bat than any man in history on May 8, 1998.

MILESTONE HOME RUNS

- McGwire becomes the first man to hit 50 homers in three consecutive seasons on August 20, 1998, against the Mets.

- McGwire crushes two homers against Florida on September 1, 1998, to pass Hank Wilson for most home runs in National League history.

- McGwire hits number 62 for the year on September 8, 1998, surpassing Maris' season record.

MILESTONE HOME RUNS

A WALK IN THE PARK

One of baseball's great signs of respect toward feared hitters is the number of Bases on Balls they are issued. Ted Williams, who was walked 20.76 times per every 100 At-Bats, the highest percentage in the history of baseball, is arguably the greatest hitter the game has ever known. Babe Ruth was third on the list, with a 19.67 percentage. Through the 1997 season, McGwire sat at number 20 on the all-time list, with a 16.20 percentage. But in 1998, shell-shocked pitchers were walking Mac at a rate of 24.65 per 100 At-Bats.

AN AVERAGE PLAYER

"I never wanted all this hoopla.
All I wanted is to be a good ball player,
hit 25 or 30 homers, drive in around a hundred runs,
hit .280 and help my club win pennants.
I just wanted to be one of the guys,
an average player having a good season."

—Roger Maris

WHAT A ROOKIE—
IT'S UNANIMOUS!

Mark McGwire was runaway winner of the 1987 Rookie of the Year Award in the American League. He is one of only 12 unanimous selections since 1947, the year the Baseball Writers' Association of America asked thirty-three writers to name the top rookie for each league.

OTHER UNANIMOUS SELECTIONS INCLUDE:

Player	Team	Year
Frank Robinson	Cincinnati Reds	1956
Orlando Cepeda	St. Louis Cardinals	1958
Willie McCovey	San Francisco Giants	1959
Carlton Fisk	Boston Red Sox	1972
Vince Coleman	New York Mets	1985
Benito Santiago	San Diego Padres	1987
Sandy Alomar	Cleveland Indians	1990
Mike Piazza	Los Angeles Dodgers	1993
Tim Salmon	California Angels	1993
Raul Mondesi	Los Angeles Dodgers	1994
Derek Jeter	New York Mets	1996

THE TOUGHEST YEARS
1991, 1993, 1994

McGwire's fifth full season in the Major Leagues, 1991, was the worst year of his career. He hit just .201, although he had a very respectable 22 homers and 75 RBIs.

His biggest struggle was adjusting to new strategies by pitchers. Plus, it seemed everyone had a suggestion on how to break out of his slump.

"I must have gotten 100 suggestions, and I listened to 90 of them."

THE TOUGHEST YEARS

In 1992, he bounced back with a .268 average, 42 home runs, and 104 RBIs. But in 1993, after a great start, he tore a tendon in his left foot. He suffered a stress fracture in the same foot during the 1994 season. All told, he hit only 18 home runs over those two seasons, missing 258 games.

BATTING AVERAGE

1.	Ty Cobb	.366	6.	Ted Williams	.344
2.	Rogers Hornsby	.358	7.	Billy Hamilton	.344
3.	Joe Jackson	.356	8.	Dan Brouthers	.342
4.	Ed Delahanty	.346	9.	Babe Ruth	.342
5.	Tris Speaker	.345	10.	Harry Heilmann	.342

#60—I GOT YOU, BABE!

McGwire caught Babe Ruth with a "Ruthian" 381-foot shot to left field off of Cincinnati Reds pitcher, Dennis Reyes, on September 5, 1998. The homer came in the Cardinals' 141st game of the season. Ruth hit number 60 on the final day of a 154-game season in 1927.

After Ruth's homer, he said to the press, "See if anybody can beat that."

Maris and McGwire did!

RUTH VS. McGWIRE

Who had the toughest road to 60 home runs? Ruth or McGwire? Here's a few good-natured arguments heard on late-night talk-sports radio programs.

Pitchers

Ruth didn't face sliders and split-finger fast balls. McGwire doesn't have to face the spitball.

Number Five Batter

Ruth had Lou Gehrig batting behind him—.373 in 1927.
McGwire has Brian Jordon or Ray Lankford behind him in 1998.

Technology

Ruth couldn't study pitchers on video. Pitchers can study McGwire on video.

Pitcher, Part 2

In Ruth's day, starting pitchers went the distance—no fresh-armed relievers. With today's league expansion, the talent pool pitching to McGwire is diluted.

RUTH VS. McGWIRE

Travel

Ruth took shorter trips—by train. More daytime baseball in the hottest part of the day, but more days off. McGwire criss-crosses the entire country by airplane.

Physical Conditions

Ruth played in smaller ballparks. McGwire hits juiced up baseballs?!

RUTH   VS.   McGWIRE

A YANKEE TRADITION

Before McGwire hit home run number 62 on September 9, 1998, a player for the Yankees had held the season home run mark for 78 years.

Babe Ruth brought the record to New York in 1920.

Trivial Pursuits

Intentional Walks to Maris in 1961?..0

Home runs by McGwire in 1998?..62

Sosa career grand slams before 1998?....................................0

Sosa grand slams in 1998?...2

McGwire grand slams in 1998?...2

Through September 8, 1998

BASEBALL STATS

500 foot home runs by McGwire in 1998? 5

Games that McGwire has hit more
than one home run in 1998? 7

Games that Sosa has hit more than
one home run in 1998? 9

Days that McGwire and Sosa have
both homered in 1998? 19

Average distance of McGwire's home runs in 1998? 428

BASEBALL STATS

HAMMERIN' HANK

The all-time home run king is Hank Aaron with 755 career round baggers in 23 seasons. But Aaron never did make it to the "50 Homer" club. His best single-season output was 44 homers, which he accomplished three times—1957, 1963, 1966. Hammerin' Hank was the model of consistency, however, hitting more than 20 home runs in 20 straight years.

Hammerin' Hank Aaron was a model of consistency, hitting at least 20 home runs in 20 straight seasons. Here he breaks Ruth's career record with homer number 715.

ANDROSTENEDIONE
AN UNFAIR ADVANTAGE?

Toward the end of McGwire's march to 62 and beyond, his use of androstenedione, an over-the-counter "dietary supplement" became a huge controversy. The NFL and International Olympic Committee banned the substance, though it is perfectly legal in Major League Baseball. Still, some wondered if this would cast a shadow over his 1998 accomplishments.

What most experts agree on is that the use of "andros" helps the athlete recover from exhaustion quicker so that he or she can work out for

a longer period of time, which perhaps has helped McGwire add muscle to his 250-pound frame.

However, no one would argue that muscle helps anyone make contact with the baseball in the first place. Despite being one of the best athletes in the world, Michael Jordan never could hit a curve ball, for example. And McGwire was already hitting home runs at a record pace long before he began using androstenedione.

The most you could argue as to the advantage McGwire has had, is that maybe he wouldn't have hit some of his home runs quite so long.

JULY FIREWORKS

Games	27	RBI	13
AB	80	BB	33
H	17	SLG	.513
HR	8	AVG	.213

POWERQUOTES

A FREAK

"He is a freak. There are power hitters, and then there is Mark McGwire. He's way beyond anybody else in this game. I've been in St. Louis 11 years, and I saw him hit more balls into the upper deck there in two months than all the other players in all my years there combined."

—Tom Pagnozzi, St. Louis Cardinal Teammate

LITTLE RED CORVETTE

In a ceremony following McGwire's 62nd home run, the St. Louis Cardinals organization presented him with a 1962 Corvette in honor of his feat.

POWERQUOTES

MAKE 'EM SAY "WOW!"

"I'd rather hit than have sex. To hit is to show strength. It's two against one at the plate, the pitcher and catcher versus you. When I'm up there, I'm thinking. 'Try everything you want. Rub up the ball. Move the fielders around. Throw me hard stuff, soft stuff. Try anything. I'm still going to hit that ball.' I love to hit that little round [ball] out of the park and make 'em say 'Wow!'"

—Reggie Jackson

MAC'S PRE-MAJOR LEAGUE STATS

USC

YEAR	G	AB	R	H	2B	3B	HR	RBI	AVG	SLG	BB	SO	SB	HR/AB
1982	29	75	14	15	2	0	3	11	.200	.347	20	15	0	25.0
1983	53	191	46	61	9	0	19	59	.319	.665	33	35	0	10.0
1984	65	237	74	92	19	2	31	77	.388	.878	30	50	2	7.6

USA Olympic Tour

YEAR	G	AB	R	H	2B	3B	HR	RBI	AVG	SLG	BB	SO	SB	HR/AB
1984	30	110	24	43	13	0	6	26	.391	.673	10	14	0	18.3

USA Olympic Games

YEAR	G	AB	R	H	2B	3B	HR	RBI	AVG	SLG	BB	SO	SB	HR/AB
1984	5	21	4	4	0	0	0	0	.190	.190	2	6	0	0.0

MINOR LEAGUES

YEAR	G	AB	R	H	2B	3B	HR	RBI	AVG	BB	SO	SB
1984	Modesto (A)	55	7	11	3	0	1	1	.200	8	21	0
1985	Modesto (A)	489	95	134	23	3	24	106	.274	96	108	1
1986	Huntsville (AA)	195	40	59	15	0	10	53	.303	46	45	3
1986	Tacoma (AAA)	280	42	89	21	5	13	59	.318	42	67	1

WHO WAS THE YOUNGEST PLAYER IN MAJOR LEAGUE BASEBALL TO HIT A HOME RUN?

Tommy "Buckshot" Brown of the Brooklyn Dodgers was seventeen years old when he hit a homer off pitcher Preacher Roe of the Pittsburgh Pirates, on August 20, 1945. He played seven more seasons in the major leagues, hitting 31 career home runs.

"Mark has power of heart
as well as power physically."

—Rod Dedeaux, McGwire's college coach at USC

THE IRON HORSE

In 1927, the year that Babe Ruth hit 60 home runs, the man batting behind him in the Yankees' lineup didn't have a bad year either. Lou Gehrig only hit .373, with 47 home runs and 175 RBIs. His RBI total is still the second highest in major league history.

INFRARED ROCKETS

Kevin Hallinan, the security chief for Major League Baseball, devised a secret marking system for the baseballs used in McGwire's games as he approached Maris' record. The purpose was to make sure that there was no question as to the authenticity of baseballs numbered 61 and 62. The markings cannot be seen by the naked eye.

The Pitch

Here's a few pitchers who will be remembered forever for home run pitches they served up:

Tom Zachary:	Babe Ruth's 60th
Tracy Stallard:	Roger Maris' 61st
Al Downing:	Hank Aaron's 715th
Eric Show:	Pete Rose's 4,123rd hit
Steve Trachsel:	Mark McGwire's 62nd
Ralph Branca:	Bobby Richardson's "shot heard 'round the world"

Unbreakable Records?

Records are made to be broken, but here are a few that probably won't be challenged any time soon:

Season Batting Average: .424	Roger Hornsby, St. Louis, 1924.
Consecutive Games with a Hit: 56	Joe DiMaggio, New York Yankees, 1941.
Consecutive Games Played: 2,596	Cal Ripken Jr., Baltimore, 1982-present.
Pitching Victories in a Season: 41	Jack Chesbro, New York, 1904.
Career Home Runs: 755	Hank Aaron, Milwaukee Atlanta Braves, 1954-1976.
RBIs in a Season: 190	Hack Wilson, Chicago Cubs, 1930.

THREE'S THE CHARM

McGwire didn't just chase Roger Maris in 1998. He attacked a number of Major League Baseball records. On August 20, he became the first player in Major League history to hit more than 50 home runs in three consecutive seasons. Babe Ruth twice hit more than 50 home runs in two consecutive seasons: 1920-1921, and 1927-1928. Hank Aaron, the all-time MLB home run champ, never reached the 50 mark for home runs in a season.

THE ROAD TO 62

On March 31, 1998, with a swing of the bat, Mark McGwire served notice to Ramon Martinez, the pitcher for the Los Angeles Dodgers that day, and the rest of the baseball world, that Roger Maris' record of 61 home runs in a single season, which had stood for 37 years, just might be in jeopardy. Ken Griffey Jr. and Sammy Sosa soon joined the hunt, but Griffey faded by late July, leaving McGwire and Sosa to battle for a spot in baseball immortality, with McGwire prevailing in the chase. Here's a sketch of his "Road to 62" compared to Roger Maris and Babe Ruth.

NO.	MARIS	McGWIRE	RUTH
1	April 26 vs. Detroit Paul Foytack	March 31 vs. Los Angeles Ramon Martinez	April 26 vs. Philadelphia Howard Ehmke
2	May 3 vs. Minnesota Pedro Ramos	April 2 vs. Los Angeles Frank Lankford	April 23 vs. Philadelphia Rube Walberg
3	May 6 at Los Angeles Eli Grba	April 3 vs. San Diego Mark Langston	April 24 vs. Washington Sloppy Thurston
4	May 17 vs. Washington Pete Burnside	April 4 vs. San Diego Don Wengert	April 29 vs. Boston Slim Hariss
5	May 19 vs. Cleveland Jim Perry	April 14 vs. Arizona Jeff Suppan	May 1 vs. Philadelphia Jack Quinn
6	May 20 vs. Cleveland Gary Bell	April 14 vs. Arizona Jeff Suppan	May 1 vs. Philadelphia Rube Walberg
7	May 21 vs. Baltimore Chuck Estrade	April 14 vs. Arizona Barry Manuel	May 10 vs. St. Louis Milt Gaston
8	May 23 vs. Boston Gene Conley	April 17 vs. Philadelphia Matt Whiteside	May 11 vs. St. Louis Ernie Nevers
9	May 28 vs. Chicago White Sox Cal McLish	April 21 vs. Montreal Trey Moore	May 17 vs. Detroit Rip H. Collins

NO.	MARIS	McGWIRE	RUTH
10	May 30 vs. Boston Gene Conley	April 25 vs. Philadelphia Jerry Spradlin	May 22 vs. Cleveland Benn Karr
11	May 30 vs. Boston Mike Fornieles	April 30 vs. Chicago Cubs Marc Pisciotta	May 23 vs. Washington Sloppy Thurston
12	May 31 vs. Boston Billy Muffett	May 1 vs. Chicago Cubs Rod Beck	May 28 vs. Washington Sloppy Thurston
13	June 2 vs. Chicago White Sox Cal Mclish	May 8 vs. New York Mets Rick Reed	May 29 vs. Boston Danny MacFayden
14	June 3 vs. Chicago White Sox Bob Shaw	May 12 vs. Milwaukee Paul Wagner	May 30 vs. Philadelphia Rube Walberg
15	June 4 vs. Chicago White Sox Russ Kemmerer	May 14 vs. Atlanta Kevin Millwood	May 31 vs. Philadelphia Jack Quinn
16	June 6 vs. Minnesota Ed Palmquist	May 16 vs. Florida Livan Hernandez	May 31 vs. Philadelphia Howard Ehmke
17	June 7 vs. Minnesota Pedro Ramos	May 18 vs. Florida Jesus Sanchez	June 5 vs. Detroit Earl Whitehill
18	June 9 vs. Kansas City Ray Herbert	May 19 vs. Philadelphia Tyler Green	June 7 vs. Chicago White Sox Tommy Thomas

NO.	MARIS	McGWIRE	RUTH
19	June 11 vs. Los Angeles Eli Grba	May 19 vs. Philadelphia Tyler Green	June 11 vs. Cleveland Garland Buckeye
20	June 11 vs. Los Angeles Johnny James	May 19 vs. Philadelphia Wayne Gomes	June 11 vs. Cleveland Garland Buckeye
21	June 13 vs. Cleveland Jim Perry	May 22 vs. San Francisco Mark Gardner	June 12 vs. Cleveland George Uhle
22	June 14 at Cleveland Gary Bell	May 23 vs. San Francisco Rich Rodriguez	June 16 vs. St. Louis Tom Zachary
23	June 17 at Detroit Don Mossi	May 23 vs. San Francisco John Johnstone	June 22 vs. Boston Hal Wiltse
24	June 18 at Detroit Jerry Casale	May 24 vs. San Francisco Robb Nen	June 22 vs. Boston Hal Wiltse
25	June 19 at Kansas City Jim Archer	May 25 vs. Colorado John Thomson	June 25 vs. Boston Slim Hariss
26	June 20 at Kansas City Joe Nuxhall	May 29 at San Diego Dan Miceli	July 3 vs. Washington Hod Lisenbee
27	June 22 at Kansas City Norm Bass	May 30 at San Diego Andy Ashby	July 8 vs. Detroit Don Hankins

NO.	MARIS	McGWIRE	RUTH
28	July 1 vs. Washington Dave Sisler	June 5 vs. San Francisco Orel Hershiser	July 9 vs. Detroit Ken Holloway
29	July 2 vs. Washington Pete Burnside	June 8 vs. Chicago White Sox Jason Bere	July 9 vs. Detroit Ken Holloway
30	July 2 vs. Washington Johnny Klippstein	June 10 vs. Chicago White Sox Jim Parque	July 12 vs. Cleveland Joe Shaute
31	July 4 vs. Detroit Frank Lary	June 12 vs. Arizona Andy Benes	July 24 vs. Chicago Tommy Thomas
32	July 5 vs. Cleveland Frank Funk	June 17 vs. Houston Jose Lima	July 26 vs. St. Louis Milt Gaston
33	July 9 vs. Boston Bill Monbouquette	June 18 vs. Houston Shane Reynolds	July 26 vs. St. Louis Milt Gaston
34	July 13 vs. Chicago White Sox Early Wynn	June 24 vs. Cleveland Jaret Wright	July 28 vs. St. Louis Lefty Stewart
35	July 15 vs. Chicago White Sox Ray Herbert	June 25 vs. Cleveland Dave Burba	August 5 vs. Detroit George S. Smith
36	July 21 vs. Boston Bill Monbouquette	June 27 vs. Minnesota Mike Trombley	August 10 vs. Washington Tom Zachary

BASEBALL STATS

NO.	MARIS	McGWIRE	RUTH
37	July 25 vs. Chicago White Sox Frank Baumann	June 30 vs. Kansas City Glendon Rusch	August 16 vs. Chicago White Sox Tommy Thomas
38	July 25 vs. Chicago White Sox Don Larsen	July 11 vs. Houston Billy Wagner	August 17 vs. Chicago White Sox Sarge Connally
39	July 25 vs. Chicago White Sox Russ Kemmerer	July 12 vs. Houston Sean Bergman	August 20 vs. Cleveland Jake Miller
40	July 25 vs. Chicago White Sox Warren Hacker	July 12 vs. Houston Scott Elarton	August 22 vs. Cleveland Joe Shaute
41	August 4 vs. Minnesota Camilo Pascual	July 17 vs. Los Angeles Brian Bohanon	August 27 vs. St. Louis Ernie Nevers
42	August 11 at Washington Pete Burnside	July 17 vs. Los Angeles Antonio Osuna	August 28 vs. St. Louis Ernie Wingard
43	August 12 at Washington Dick Donovan	July 20 vs. San Diego Brian Boehringer	August 31 vs. Boston Tony Welzer
44	August 13 at Washington Bernie Daniels	July 26 at Colorado John Thomson	September 2 vs. Philadelphia Rube Walberg
45	August 13 at Washington Marty Kutyna	July 28 vs. Milwaukee Mike Myers	September 6 vs. Boston Tony Welzer

NO.	MARIS	McGWIRE	RUTH
46	August 15 vs. Chicago White Sox Juan Pizarro	August 8 vs. Chicago Cubs Mark Clark	September 6 vs. Boston Tony Welzer
47	August 16 vs. Chicago White Sox Billy Pierce	August 11 vs. New York Mets Bobby Jones	September 6 vs. Boston Jack Russell
48	August 16 vs. Chicago White Sox Billy Pierce	August 19 at Chicago Cubs Matt Karchner	September 7 vs. Boston Danny MacFayden
49	August 20 at Cleveland Jim Perry	August 19 at Chicago Cubs Terry Mulholland	September 7 vs. Boston Slim Harriss
50	August 22 at Los Angeles Ken McBride	August 20 at New York Mets Willie Blair	September 11 vs. St. Louis Milt Gaston
51	August 26 at Kansas City Jerry Walker	August 20 at New York Mets Rick Reed	September 13 vs. Cleveland Willis Hudlin
52	September 2 vs. Detroit Frank Lary	August 22 at Pittsburgh Francisco Cordova	September 13 vs. Cleveland Joe Shaute
53	September 2 vs. Detroit Hank Aguirre	August 23 at Pittsburgh Ricardo Rincon	September 16 vs. Chicago White Sox Ted Blankenship
54	September 6 vs. Washington Tom Cheney	August 26 vs. Florida Justin Speier	September 18 vs. Chicago White Sox Ted Lyons

BASEBALL STATS

NO.	MARIS	McGWIRE	RUTH
55	September 7 vs. Cleveland Dick Stigman	August 30 vs. Atlanta Dennis Martinez	September 21 vs. Detroit Sam Gibson
56	September 9 at Cleveland Mudcat Grant	September 1 vs. Florida Livan Hernandez	September 22 vs. Detroit Ken Holloway
57	September 16 at Detroit Frank Lary	September 1 vs. Florida Donn Pall	September 27 vs. Philadelphia Lefty Grove
58	September 17 at Detroit Terry Fox	September 2 vs. Florida B. Edmondson	September 29 vs. Washington Hod Lisenbee
59	September 20 at Baltimore Milt Pappas	September 2 vs. Florida Rob Standifer	September 29 vs. Paul Hopkins
60	September 26 vs. Baltimore Jack Fisher	September 5 vs. Cincinnati Dennis Reyes	September 30 vs. Washington Tom Zachary
61	October 1 vs. Boston Tracy Stallard	September 7 vs. Chicago Cubs Mike Morgan	
62		September 8 vs. Chicago Cubs Steve Trachsel	

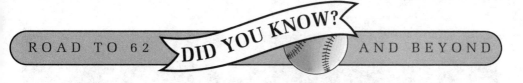
A GOLDEN GLOVE, TOO!

McGwire won the Golden Glove Award for first basemen in the American league in 1990. Who knows how many he might have won had the competition not been so stiff at his position. The year he won, McGwire ended a five year winning streak by Don Mattingly, affectionately known in New York as "Donny Baseball." Mattingly, of the New York Yankees, went on to win the Golden Glove Award the next four years as well. It just so happens that Mattingly has the second highest fielding percentage among first basemen in the history of Major League Baseball, behind only Steve Garvey.

Even sluggers have to back down at times—
especially when a 95-mile-per-hour fastball sails inside.

POWERQUOTES

"I remember when Hank was going for 715, and they nationally televised all his games. I remember sitting in the living room watching it, and it was a great feeling as a kid. If I get there or somebody else gets there in a nationally televised game, I'm sure some young kid is going to feel what I felt."

—Mark McGwire

DID YOU KNOW?

In 1996, McGwire homered once every 8.13 at-bats, beating Babe Ruth's mark of homering once every 8.48 at-bats, set in 1920. In 1997, McGwire homered onced every 9.31 at-bats, the fifth best in major league history. But in 1998, McGwire topped even himself, hitting a home run every 7.6 at-bats.

THE BIG HACK ATTACK

In 1998, McGwire and Sosa caught and surpassed the Cubs' Hack Wilson's National League record of 56 home runs in 1930—a record that stood for 68 years. Wilson's Major League record of 190 runs batted in, appears to be safe for another year. The only serious challenges to that amazing mark were mounted by Lou Gehrig with 184 in 1931, and Hank Greenberg with 183 in 1937.

Some baseball historians note that Wilson's record came during the year of the "live ball." The batting average of all players in the National League that year was .303. Six of the eight teams batted higher than .300. Philadelphia hit .319 as a team, a record that will probably never be broken. Seventy-one players hit .300 or better that year!

The Maris Line

Name at Birth:	Roger Eugene Maras*
Birthplace:	Hibbing, Minnesota
Raised:	Fargo, North Dakota
Vital Stats:	6', 204 pounds
Died:	December 14, 1985, in Houston, Texas
Position:	Right Field
Batted:	Left
Teams:	Cleveland Indians, Kansas City Athletics, New York Yankees, St. Louis Cardinals
Awards:	American League MVP in 1960 and 1961

Career Numbers: 1,465 games

5,101 At-Bats

1,325 hits

275 home runs

851 runs batted in

.260 batting average

* When asked why he changed the spelling of his name, Maris answered, "It's immaterial."

Seasons With Two or More Players Hitting 50 Homers

1998—Mark McGwire (62), Sammy Sosa (58), and Ken Griffey Jr. (50)

1997—Mark McGwire (58) and Ken Griffey Jr. (56)

1996—Mark McGwire (52) and Brady Anderson (50)

1961—Roger Maris (61) and Mickey Mantle (54)

1947—Ralph Kiner (51) and Johnny Mize (51)

*and counting!

THE MIDST OF THE STORM

Because of his "audacity" in attacking Ruth's record, Maris was booed and taunted everywhere he played, including home. The pressure by fans and media became so intense that Maris' hair began to fall out in clumps. It was often reported that he and Mickey Mantle, also in the chase for 60 that year until a late-season injury ended his bid, were feuding. The press didn't know that they were roomates.

In the midst of the storm, Maris simply kept hitting homers.

AUGUST HEAT

Games	28	RBI	19
AB	90	BB	31
H	26	SLG	.700
HR	10	AVG	.289

#61—HELLO ROGER

McGwire blasted a pitch from the Cubs' Mike Morgan 430 feet to left field in the first inning of the Cardinals-Cubs game on September, 7, tying Maris' hallowed mark that has stood for 37 years.

McGwire's homer came on the Cardinals' 144th game of the season. Maris hit number 61 on the last day of a 162-game season.

McGwire's 10-year-old son, Matthew, was waiting for his dad at home plate, and received a bear hug from "the Big Mac."

Two Cubs players gave McGwire high fives as he circled the bases— first baseman Mark Grace, and former St. Louis teammate Gary Gaetti, third baseman for the Cubs.

HAPPY 61st!

"What a birthday!"

That's what John McGwire declared after his son, slugger Mark McGwire, gift-wrapped home run number 61 on his father's 61st birthday.

JAPAN'S "SULTAN OF SWAT"

Sadaharu Oh of the Tokyo Giants, still holds the record for the most home runs in a career, with 868. From 1965-1973, Oh led the Giants to victory in nine straight Japan Series. Oh played only 130 games a year, and was walked so often, that he often came up to bat fewer than 300 times. Most Major League Baseball home run champs have historically had more than 500 At-Bats.

GEORGE HERMAN "BABE" RUTH

Babe Ruth began his career as a left-handed pitcher for the Boston Red Sox in 1914. He compiled a 78-40 record in four years with the Red Sox.

Ruth became a full time outfielder in 1919, setting a new home run record of 29 and leading the league in runs, RBI's, and slugging percentage.

He led the league in home runs eight of the next ten years.

GEORGE HERMAN "BABE" RUTH

Ruth led the league in home runs 12 times, runs 8 times, RBI's 6 times, and slugging percentage 13 times during his twenty full seasons.

Ruth's lifetime batting average was .342.

He was the all time leader in home run percentages (11.8) until McGwire caught him in 1998, walks (2056), and slugging percentage (.690).

Ruth was one of the first five elected to the Hall of Fame in 1936, receiving 95% of the votes possible (215 out of 226).

GEORGE   HERMAN   "BABE"   RUTH

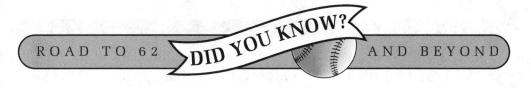

FANS BOYCOTT MARIS
What a difference 37 years can make.

The New York Yankees, an exciting team on its way to a World Series show-down with the Cincinnati Reds, had clinched the American League pennant in a tough playoff race in 1961. You would expect huge crowds as Maris approached Ruth's record.

But because New York never warmed to Maris, the 1960 American League MVP, and because many definitely were not excited about him breaking what was considered to be an unbreakable record, barely 23,000 spectators showed up on October 1, 1961, to see his historic blast.

Though the 1998 Cardinals never made a run at the playoffs, and were sitting in 3rd place with a 70-73 record at this time, because of McGwire's local—and national—popularity, a sell-out crowd of 43,688 witnessed his breaking of Maris' record against the Cubs on September 8, 1998.

WHO DID THE A's GET?

On July 31, 1997, having already hit 34 home runs for the season, the Athletics traded McGwire to St. Louis for three pitchers. What kind of careers have they had so far?

Eric Ludwick   Starting Pitcher
Florida, Marlins/traded for IF Kurt Abbott on December 19, 1997
6'5", 210 pounds

1998 Statistics

W-L	SAVES	ERA	GAMES	IP	Ks	BBs
1-3	0	5.90	9	29	25	14

T. J. Mathews   Relief Pitcher
Oakland Athletics
6'2", 200 pounds

1998 Statistics

W-L	SAVES	ERA	GAMES	IP	Ks	BBs
5-4	1	4.38	58	61.2	47	26

Blake Stein   Starting Pitcher
Oakland Athletics
6'7", 210 pounds

1998 Statistics

W-L	SAVES	ERA	GAMES	IP	Ks	BBs
5-8	0	6.36	20	109	79	64

BASEBALL STATS

#62! A LEAGUE OF HIS OWN

It happened at 8:18 p.m. in St. Louis.

He grounded out on a 3-0 count his first time at bat.

Now with two outs in the fourth inning, he swung at Steve Trachsel's first pitch and drove it 341 feet—his shortest homer of the year—for the biggest record in all of baseball history!

The crowd of 43,688 roared in approval. Even the opposing Cubs, in the thick of a race for the National League's wild card play-off berth, didn't hold back their cheers.

'98 POWERSHOTS

Sammy Sosa, who raced all year to break Maris' mark, trotted in from right field to give McGwire a celebratory hug.

In a brief mid-inning speech, McGwire thanked his family, his son, the Cubs, Sosa—and St. Louis.

'98 POWERSHOTS

MATTHEW

Though McGwire may have missed an opportunity to hit 50 home runs in his rookie year to be present for the birth of his son, it is Matthew that has been one of Mac's greatest inspirations on the road to 62. The ten-year-old is bat boy for the Cardinals and has a reserved seat on the team plane for all away games that he is able to attend with his dad. Matthew received a bear hug at home plate in front of a worldwide television audience when his dad hit home run number 61.

REGGIE! REGGIE! REGGIE!

The man who was supposed to break Roger Maris' record for home runs was known by friends and foes alike as "Mr. October," for his World Series feats. In 1969, Reggie Jackson pounded out 37 home runs for the Oakland Athletics before the All Star break, and looked to be a shoe-in to surpass Maris and the Babe in the record books. But Jackson, one of baseball's great clutch performers of all time, eked out only 10 more homers during the second half of the season, ending the year with 47 round baggers.

Kiss It Goodbye

FAVORITE PHRASES BY ANNOUNCERS WHEN A HOME RUN IS HIT:

"Bye-bye baby."
—Russ Hodges

"Forget it."
—Vin Scully

"Goodbye, baseball!"
—Dick Risenhoover

"Goodbye, Dolly Grey."
—Leo Durocher

"Open the window, Aunt Minnie, here it comes."
—Rosey Roswell

"Tell it goodbye!"
—Jon Miller

"That ball is history."
—Eric Nagel

"They usually show movies on a flight like that."
—Ken Coleman

*"Whoo, boy! Next time around,
bring me back my stomach."*
—Jack Brickhouse

McGWIRE THROUGH THE YEARS!

Professional Career Satistics as of September 8, 1998

Year	Club	Avg.	Games	At-Bats	Runs	Hits	Doubles
1986	Oakland	.189	18	53	10	10	1
1987	Oakland	.289	151	557	97	161	28
1988	Oakland	.260	155	550	87	143	22
1989	Oakland	.231	143	490	74	113	17
1990	Oakland	.235	156	523	87	123	16
1991	Oakland	.201	154	483	62	97	22
1992	Oakland	.268	139	467	87	125	22
1993	Oakland	.333	27	84	16	28	6
1994	Oakland	.252	47	135	26	34	3
1995	Oakland	.274	104	317	75	87	13
1996	Oakland	.312	130	423	104	132	21
1997	Oakland	.284	105	366	48	104	24
	St. Louis	.253	51	174	38	44	3
1998	St. Louis	.267	136	449	115	133	19

BASEBALL STATS

MAJOR LEAGUE TOTALS

Year	Triples	Homers	RBI	BB	SO	Stolen Bases
1987	4	49	118	71	131	1
1988	1	32	99	76	117	0
1989	0	33	95	83	94	1
1990	0	39	108	110	116	2
1991	0	22	75	93	116	2
1992	0	42	104	90	105	0
1993	0	9	24	21	19	0
1994	0	9	25	37	40	0
1995	0	39	90	88	77	1
1996	0	52	113	116	112	0
1997	0	34	81	58	98	1
	0	24	42	43	61	2
1998	0	62	129	149	137	1

HITS

1.	Pete Rose	4,256	6.	Carl Yastrzemski	3,419
2.	Ty Cobb	4,189	7.	Honus Wagner	3,415
3.	Hank Aaron	3,771	8.	Eddie Collins	3,315
4.	Stan Musial	3,630	9.	Willie Mays	3,283
5.	Tris Speaker	3,514	10.	Nap Lajoie	3,242

MCGWIRE AND ADVERTISERS

At this point in his career, McGwire has turned down all offers to endorse products.

That's how many athletes make the lion's share of their money, but McGwire says:

"I want to play baseball. That's the first concern of mine. I would rather get my exposure on TV playing the game of baseball."

McGwire's home run tear has transformed him into a highly popular player with memorabilia hunters over the last few years!

	Summer 1994	Summer 1998
Signed Baseball	$30	$65
Signed Photo	$20	$55
Signed Bat	$129	$175
Game-used bat	$300	$795
Game-used jersey	$1,250	$1,500

FANS IN THE STANDS

The St. Louis Cardinals are not contending for a playoff spot in 1998, but with McGwire on the team, attendance at the ballpark has skyrocketed both at home for the Cardinals and on the road. St. Louis's attendance is expected to reach a major league-leading 3.2 million in 1998.

Despite capturing two consecutive MVP awards in the American League, Maris has never been elected to baseball's Hall of Fame.

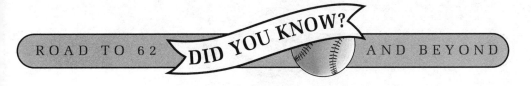
13 YEARS LATER

Thirteen years after Babe Ruth died, Roger Maris broke his home run record for a season with a fourth inning homer.

Thirteen years after Roger Maris died, Mark McGwire broke his home run record for a season with a fourth inning home run.

CAREER HIGHLIGHTS AT A GLANCE

Rookie record for home runs in a season (49)

Unanimous 1987 AL Rookie of the Year

American League Golden Glove, in 1990 at first base

Led the Major Leagues in home runs four times: 1987, 1996, 1997, 1998

National League record for home runs in a season: 1998

POWERQUOTES

MAX IT OUT

"Mark hits it farther with less effort than anyone ever. It's timing, and it's a gift not everybody has. He reaches the ball at the exact moment when he can max it out."

—Tony La Russa, McGwire's manager in Oakland and St. Louis

THE RUTH LEGACY

Few athletes captured the imagination of the masses like Babe Ruth—perhaps Muhammad Ali and Michael Jordan, but few others.

Ruth was so well known internationally that during World War II, when Japanese soldiers wanted to taunt Americans across the battle lines, they would shout: "To hell with Babe Ruth."

GEORGE HERMAN "BABE" RUTH

Ruth was one of only two people (Reggie Jackson being the other) to ever hit three home runs in a World Series game and is the only one to do it twice (1926 & 1928).

Ruth is credited with the invention of the modern baseball bat. He was the first player to order a bat with a knob on the end of the handle. Louisville Slugger produced the bat with which he hit 29 home runs in 1919.

Ruth holds the record for the longest complete game victory in World Series history. In 1916, as a member of the Boston Red Sox, Ruth went 14 innings to defeat the New York Giants 2-1.

GEORGE HERMAN "BABE" RUTH

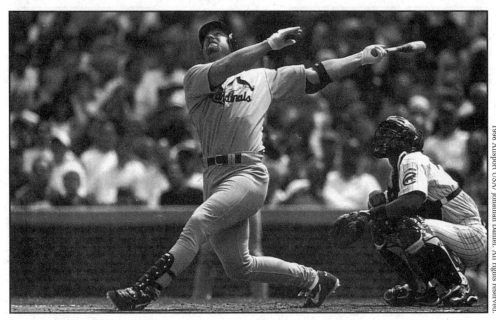

McGwire takes a mighty swing toward 62!

POWERQUOTES

MAAARRRRRRRRRRK!

"We had like a two and a half hour wait after a game in Philadelphia because our plane was delayed, and we waited in the clubhouse. And even after two-and-a-half hours, there must have been 1,000 people standing outside where our bus was. And I mean it was just like, 'Maaaarrrrrrk, Maaaarrrrrrk, Maaaarrrrrrk.' He's the fifth Beatle. You've got John, Paul, George, Ringo and Mark."

—Cardinals third baseman Gary Gaetti, who was later traded to the Cubs.

BEYOND 62!

**Keep track of all Mark McGwire's
home runs past 62 in 1998.**

No.	Date	Team	Pitcher
63			
64			
65			
66			

BEYOND 62!

No.	Date	Team	Pitcher
67			
68			
69			
70			

ENDNOTES

30. Quoted in *The Sporting News,* Dec 15, 1997 v221 n50 p14(7), Kindred, Dave.

37. Quoted in *Hammerin' Hank* by Dan Schlossberg.

38. Quoted by Thomas R. Raber, *St. Louis Magazine,* April 1998, p.33.

41. Quoted in *The Sporting News,* Dec 15, 1997 v221 n50 p14(7) Kindred, Dave.

58. Barry M. Bloom, *Sport,* August 1998, p. 72.

59. Quoted by William Safire and Leonard Safir in *Words of Wisdom.*

79. Quoted by Jack Orr in *My Greatest Day in Baseball.*

99. *Time Magazine,* June 3, 1974.

103. *Time Magazine,* July 27, 1998 p. 40.

119. From *Sunday Conversations with Peter Gammons* on ESPN.

140-41. Paul Dickson, *Baseball's Greatest Quotations.* Harper Collins, 1991, pp. 185-86.

145. Quoted by Thomas R. Raber, *St. Louis Magazine,* April 1998, pp. 35-36.

McGWIRE'S FUND FOR CHILDREN

A portion of all proceedes from this book will go to the McGwire Fund for Children.

The Publisher encourages all readers to contribute to this charity by sending a check to:

Cardinals Kids/Busch Stadium
256 Stadium Plaza
St. Louis, MO 63102-1722

Please make checks payable to Dr. Ed Lewis and in the memo section write: Mark McGwire Foundation.